A desert can be hot in the day and cold at night. It almost never rains, so the desert is also dry. Even so, many animals and their babies live there.

Desert Tortoise Babies

Desert tortoise babies hatch out of eggs. The mother lays only one or two eggs at a time. She does not touch her eggs again.

An interesting thing happens to
the tortoises in the eggs. In warm sand,
they turn into female tortoises. In cool
sand, they turn into male tortoises. After
hatching, the babies go under the sand
to stay cool.

Bighorn Sheep Babies

When a bighorn sheep baby is born, it stays with its mother for a few weeks. The mother takes care of the baby. She protects it from other animals.

Soon the baby will group together with other bighorn sheep babies. The babies only go back to their mothers to drink milk.

Roadrunner Babies

Roadrunners are small birds. They may build their nest in a prickly cactus or a bush. This keeps the eggs safe. When the roadrunner babies hatch, they are hungry.

First, the parents make the babies drink water. The water comes from the parent's stomach. It trickles into the baby's mouth. After the baby drinks the water, the mother or father feeds the baby food.

Spadefoot Toad Babies

Spadefoot toads live under the ground for most of the year. They do this to stay cool. When it rains, the toads come out of the ground to mate. Then the female toad lays eggs in pools of water.

Tadpoles

Soon the eggs hatch into tadpoles.
They are much smaller than your thumb.
The tadpoles change quickly into toads
before the pools dry up. Before long, the
baby toads go under the ground, too.
They may not appear again for months!

Jackrabbit Babies

Jackrabbits are really hares. Jackrabbit babies are born above ground. They have fur and their eyes are open. Jackrabbit babies are able to move around soon after they are born.

A jackrabbit mother hides each of her babies in a different place. Then she goes off to feed. On her way back, she searches for her babies by calling to them. They answer her, and she finds them quickly.

Life can be hard in the desert, but it is home to many animals and their babies.

Think Critically

1. What happens to the babies in the eggs of a desert tortoise?

2. What happens before the baby roadrunner is given food by its mother or father?

3. What is something both the spadefoot toad and desert tortoise babies will do?

4. How can you tell this is a nonfiction book?

5. If you had the chance to see one of the desert babies, which one would you choose? Why?

 Science

Group the Animals Draw two boxes on a sheet of paper and write one of these headings in each box: *Hatches from an Egg, Does not Hatch from an Egg*. Write the names of the animals from the book in the correct boxes. Draw your favorite desert baby.

School-Home Connection Discuss the pictures in *Desert Babies* with a family member. Talk about what it would be like to live in the desert.

Desert Babies

by Elise Petrie

SCHOOL PUBLISHERS

Cover (background) ©Harcourt Index; (main) ©Photolibrary.com; 3 ©Photolibrary.com; 4 ©Bruce Coleman Inc.; 5–6 ©Photolibrary.com; 7 ©Getty Images; 8–9 ©Rolf Nussbaumer/Nature Picture Library; 10 ©Photolibrary.com; 11 ©John Cancalosi/Nature Picture Library; 12 ©Photolibrary.com; 13 ©Telescope Web; 14 (tl) ©Photolibrary.com; (tr) ©Photolibrary.com; (bl) ©Bruce Coleman Inc.; (br) ©Rolf Nussbaumer/Nature Picture Library.

Printed in Mexico

ISBN 10: 0-15-350647-4
ISBN 13: 978-0-15-350647-5

Ordering Options
ISBN 10: 0-15-350599-0 (Grade 2 On-Level Collection)
ISBN 13: 978-0-15-350599-7 (Grade 2 On-Level Collection)
ISBN 10: 0-15-357828-9 (package of 5)
ISBN 13: 978-0-15-357828-1 (package of 5)

4 5 6 7 8 9 10   050   15 14 13 12 11 10 09 08